WORMWOOD

Also by Ken Smith

The Pity (Jonathan Cape, 1967)
Work, distances/poems (Swallow Press, Chicago, 1972)
Tristan Crazy (Bloodaxe Books, 1978)
Fox Running (Bloodaxe Books, 1981)
Burned Books (Bloodaxe Books, 1981)
Abel Baker Charlie Delta Epic Sonnets (Bloodaxe Books, 1982)
The Poet Reclining: Selected Poems (Bloodaxe Books, 1982)
Terra (Bloodaxe Books, 1986)
A Book of Chinese Whispers (Bloodaxe Books, 1987)

WORMWOOD

KEN SMITH

BLOODAXE BOOKS

ISBN: 1 85224 037 7

First published 1987 by
Bloodaxe Books Ltd,
P.O. Box 1SN,
Newcastle upon Tyne NE99 1SN.

Bloodaxe Books Ltd acknowledges
the financial assistance of Northern Arts.

Typesetting by Bryan Williamson, Manchester.

Printed in Great Britain by
Bell & Bain Limited, Glasgow, Scotland.

For Jessica

And the name of the star is called Wormwood: and the third part of the waters became wormwood; and many men died of the waters, because they were made bitter.

REVELATIONS 8.2

All other wormwoods, the nearer they approach in taste to pleasant and palatable, they are so much the worse, for they are weaker, their use requires so much longer time, larger doses, and yet less success follows.

NICHOLAS CULPEPER

Some notes

From September 1985 to August 1987 I was writer-in-residence to Her Majesty's Prison, Wormwood Scrubs, where my work was mostly with life sentence inmates of D Wing. These are the poems I wrote during the first 18 months of this period of my life, and here I wish to thank many people: Greater London Arts, who funded the fellowship, together with Ilea; the Governor and staff of the prison for their help, advice, and tolerance in allowing me access and considerable freedom of movement within the prison; the Education Officer, teachers and other prison workers who smoothed and guided my path; and the many prisoners with whom I worked and who opened their closed worlds to me. To all of these I am deeply grateful, especially to: Des, Ross, Len, Jim, Bob, H, Fuzzy, John, Col, Derek, Robb, Phil, Dave, Billy, and others who are nameless only here.

Wormwood is the name of a herb said to have grown on the Scrubs from which the prison takes its name. Locals were said to have made beer from it. It is also known as Green Ginger, and is used in the making of absinthe. It contains a hallucinogen, serotonin, which accounts for the reputation of absinthe drinkers and its absence in this country from the off licence shelves.

Wormwood is also the name of the star in Revelations whose falling ushers in Armageddon. Shortly after the Chernobyl disaster an item appeared in the *Daily Telegraph* claiming that Russians were turning to their Bibles disturbed that, in Russian, Chernobyl means Wormwood, denoting an area formerly grown over by it. But *cherno* in Russian means *black*, and Chernobyl *place that was black*. Subsequently the bishop of Kiev wrote to the Telegraph asking that the story be denied, since it was a lie, and any panic in the Ukraine had only come about as a result of the story, whose source is no doubt the CIA, which now has a department that invents jokes.

Time is what it is appeared as a line of graffiti on the top of a cardboard desk in a cell in the segregation unit. Whoever had written it had done so in a slow careful way that suggested he had fully grasped the meaning and all the tonal possibilities of the phrase.

This is a commercial: there will be a prose book, *Inside Time*, written as a collaboration between myself and several of the men on D wing.

Acknowledgements

Acknowledgements are due to the editors of the following publications in which some of these poems have appeared: *Ambit, Antaeus* (New York), *Harry's Hand, London Magazine, Numbers, Poetry Book Society Anthology 1986/87* and *1987/88* (Hutchinson/PBS, 1986 & 1987), *Poetry Review, Relations* (Belgrade), and *The Rialto*. 'Wormwood', the proem and the picture, are taken from *The Backyard Herbal* by Ken Smith and Judi Benson.

Contents

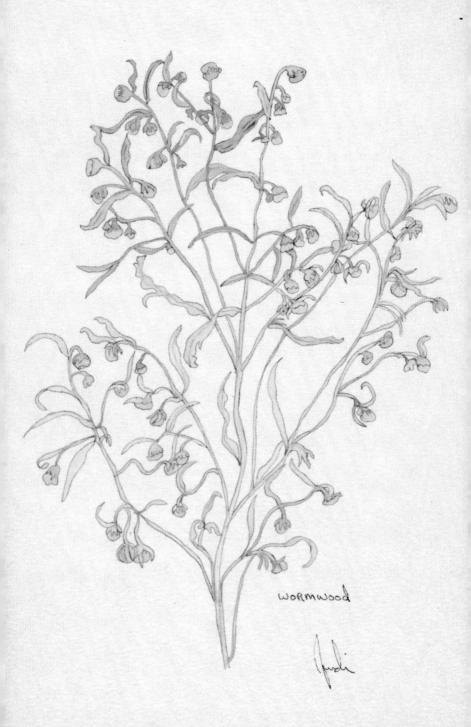

WORMWOOD

Wormwood

Down and more down. Down the ladders and down the snakes and never passing Go, never winning the state lottery nor so much as the Christmas raffle, never throwing double six, never dreaming of the winner in the 2.30 at Cheltenham, never finding sixpence in the plum pudding. There was never any luck that was good. And so down the steps in chains and down the stairs in cuffs, and backwards down the up escalator shackled to the jailer, and at last in a bodybag down the well under the cellar under the basement under the crypt under the undercroft and still some down to go.

So here I am, drinking the green absinthe of my wounds, weary from descent, from falling, drinking to get drunk. Enough of it and I'll be crazy and forget everything, I'll be wide open and talking aloud to myself or anyone or no one about the yellow dust, the ragged leaves, the palest green, the serotonin.

I dreamed you were not who I thought. You were at the airport opening your passport to another identity, a name I was not familiar with: *Jessica. Jessica Snow.* You were who you were before I knew you; you were who you are without me; you were who you are anyway. Your look said *But I am always Jessica. Always have been. Always will be.* You were leaving, going home to your own country one way without thought of return to answer old letters and the questions of old lovers, to look through shoes and coats still hanging in the closets, mementos in drawers. You were a stranger in my life, I in yours: someone I never knew on a long vacation under another name, the one I knew you by. You were a country only visiting mine in another country I only visited with you.

Artemesia absinthum: yard high and wildly divided. Curer of worms and quinsy and the bites of.rats and mice, vile and bitter, beauty's name for solace. Opaque, iced, sweetened through silver, I drink to her, to Artemis, *destitute of delight.*

For Nicki in December

I walked by the sea,
for the last time by this sea.
Give up your dead I said.

No dead came ashore on the white
lines of water, by the white stones.

Not the knife that cuts
but the hand holding the knife.
Not the sea but its element
– hostile, bearing no ill will –
drowns us, she said.

I walked a long time.
No dead came ashore.

Mine are the cleanest dead
she said
she said.

Airport silences
(for Friedermann)

On the eighth day whiteout, the 747s
ghost vague and mist drenched
and like us grounded. *Fog* they say.
Announcements will be announced.

So much promise in departure.
So little comfort in promise.

A drink, friend, let's talk
in the last of this currency
minted from courage and silence,
let's talk about weather.

From my American period

Point is friend, you & I
we don't go much further together.

Either the whisky dislikes us
or we smoke different brands.

And the landscape's brutal, repetitious,
with no deposit on the empties.

Or maybe just my horse
don't like your horse.

B

Fun City encore

On the headland wind and the wide sea,
as above: boat distant, gulls, sky,
beaded spray on the leaves of the grass,
at my feet its wild stitchery.

And these old graves, stones
wind has scribbled the names from:
Messrs Grimgrind and Whingeon
still bleating their unpaid accounts.

Thereafter the relatives.
They moan like the North Sea wind,
generations that shoulder complaint
on and on in the grey sea weather.

But the battery's flat at last
in the plastic parrot by the amusements,
and the bingo caller's throat's been cut
at the pier's end. At long last.

The rope

Away in some northerly distance
remote province a far interior
my heart's royal ancient republic

hunched across thin upland wind
chilly fields rainy sky that darkens
inking the rolling table of moorland

drum tight to such effort
a man folding a fist of himself
drags his rope through rain-heavy bracken

in case he may need it:
cable he coils out of himself
into more distance he's crossed.

Such a length of hawser that man I was
stoney pasture his cold country
over the treeline of linnet sound

windy holdings nailed to the ridges
hard bitter soils black as a raven
stones set to keep track of stars

he considers *for no particular purpose*
him with his rope he drags after
in case he finds use for it

when he can't even hang himself
not with the braid of his blood
not with the skin he was born in

nor the long skin he will die in
nor the blue coil of the umbilical
connecting him to anyone who ever loved him.

*

Whoever I was once
a boy that began tangling string
I was never innocent from the start
everyone my toy everyone my tuppence.

This phase lasted far too long.
Fists knives a black metalleta
the ink green eyes of the Guardia Civil
in the iron city of Bilbao convinced me.

We are real as the rain and die
we are as brief we are what hungers
wondering at the stars each one
the nail sharp eye of the universe.

Where is one great tatter of string
all my days have become unravelling
or more ravelling. I take one thread
it runs back in the same labyrinth.

Back into the museum of marriages
along the clogged thread of weddings
she and I each other's business
each the other's final telegram.

Each other's audience each other's movie
who might have been anyone at all
wanderers in the city with everyone
a separate event more often lonely.

Now if it ever comes out this string
it is the bare light shedding back
off stars spreading into separate distance
and the long rope ends in a noose.

A seawrack of ropes snagged up
lines grafted with other lines
the last a drowned sailor held
as the wave shocked breath out of him.

Nothing now but faulty connections
the deep ocean cable burned out
the continents no more in touch
than she I was wifed with and I were.

*

I am awake who was asleep and dreaming
the dark water he will drown in,
the rope that will hang him at last.

In a 3 a.m. city of clocks, the traffic's
horizon note or the first sleepy bird cries
or a scream woke me that might be my own.

I had dreamed ships rigged on the winds,
the last ropes slipped from the quays
down the long stones of my imagining.

And I falling with them, the light
the good star makes thinned underwater,
the coiled sea tightened till it woke me.

At the rope's end there's no rope.
I'm falling away with my hands burning
into a world at the world's end.

Where the black nib dribbles its ink
down the casualty lists, the transistor
whispering news from all the warfronts.

I am where I feared where the ocean
has washed us all ashore, I am
with others at the end of things, goodbye.

And mine is a black song brothers,
a book of the many bladed rain
but the long rope comes out here.

Where I open the buttons of my shirt,
where I keep the black rainbow
tattooed over the space of my heart.

Serbian letters
(for Ioan Flora)

I

I'm back from wherever: highways
twisted through mountains, the road
of the armies, the caravan trail
down to Istanbul dumping flotsam
and camel dung. There the river
sent me one dark caress, one glimpse
of a woman's white face and her hands
through leaves and the rain. Again,
we're surprised each time by autumn,
the trees shedding their ribbons,
rainy flags of the corn fodder,
upright fist of some fortress
raised in the mist. *In the mountains
a small dark people*, I read now
in my notes, in my mind the rain
still falling, the patriarch saying
look what our fathers have done.

II

So then I got lost explaining
how I got lost, I would be all day
writing my message to myself,
I with a thirst no drink slakes
in the dark city. *Nema problema.*
We were having literary evenings,
discussions followed by general
fuckings, speakings in tongues,
moments of silence, brain damage.
So how are you my brother,
we meet in a dangerous season,
my sister? I recall how we peered
through the bars of cyrillic
to find water, finding you
peering back: through the bars
of the alphabets, through the bars
of Belgrade singing *Jerusalem.*

III

On the seventh day of singing,
on the sixth day of laughing,
a man fell from the fifth floor
dead at my feet in a sheet but
his last breath blew through me
with all the bad air of the city.
This was the last day. He jumped
down the air with our voices
last to next door in his skull,
now I bear him a little way on.
The rest was parts put together,
drinking toasts, declaring *stop*
hunger stop war stop bomb stop
to the actors without shadows,
the smooth-suited, the well-fed.
Miodrag or Pedrag, he jumped
down the world's well. Share him.

IV

Bear with me brother once more
the long ride to Novi Pazar,
the white sheets of the mists,
the rough landscapes of grief:
wild Illyria, scree black, scrub
red with autumn, heaped windfalls,
black fruit, black flowers
of the mountain. We remember:
the halftrucks fallen in,
troops, bullets, those taken
to be lettered in stones,
names that never give in: *Adam,*
Jordan, Stepan. We'll pull wild
mountain thyme, we'll be half goat
half singing in the tall air,
your words through our mouths,
our mouths through your words.

V

There was the error: the telephone
singing in a locked room. There
where I was standing on my hands,
words squealing under my bootsoles.
There was the world in a mirror,
the words upside down, the lettering
bars of light in the darkness. We
have no proper study of failure,
we merely grow used to it. There
in the dark town of minarets
where the lists were reversed,
the dead counted living, the missing
listed as dead with the quick.
And worse nightmare: the glass
said *cut*, the window said *jump*.
I'm alive to deny it. There, sister,
my last encounter with darkness.

VI

Maybe somebody lost the key,
maybe it's world war three.
These were our *Balkan Nights,
Balkan Time*. We were having
Rumania said *A Scotch Affair*,
drunk again, where we'll all
go together. The Poles smoked,
the Russians were circumspect,
the Czechs quietly intelligent.
We spoke of the neuro-surgeon,
an open minded man, we think
that's a beginning, him sitting
on the bus with a knife in him.
Tell the president I'm gun-shy,
tell the Greeks I surrender.
·And turn off the camera, whose
movie is this we're appearing in?

VII

This for the Greeks and my sisters:
why should you ever forgive us –
my countrymen, cousins, uncles,
my brothers the conscripts firing
into the square, so many we left
smashed on the stones in the red
red ropes of an autumn of blood.
So soon all we recall in the blur
of roadsides is so many trees
that were squabbles of starlings,
windy leaves at the year's last.
So long in the moon's shadow,
now it's too late. In my own
chilly northern country the gates
slither shut in the prison house.
So let's dance. So let's sing.
Let's be one tribe made of many.

VIII

Home again in the enterprise zone.
Am I looking down a telescope
or is it the barrel of a gun
or a rolled sheet of paper this
letter is written on? Innocence
I've some remembrance of, some yarn
the slow wind tells itself
among birches. I light a candle
for Miodrag or Pedrag, you also.
Now there's small lights burning
east west, in distant cities
where the desklamps hood the paper,
the words come, letter by letter:
peace and to eat. So who cares
what the birds call themselves
or what the grass sings? I'm well,
friend, trusting this finds you so.

A theme of razors

1

One cut and the blood rings:
Roland's horn running in the mountains,
the dark Vascos inching rocks to ambush
manoeuvre through the deadfalls.

Some nights the clock's hand will not sleep,
night rides her cargo out at anchor
on the tide's approaches, and the blood
is thumping out its message to the pillow:

*you will die, your heart
imploding like a busted TV.*

You hear the static in the phone.
The drum of waves ashore.
The ticking out of every grain of sand.
The itch inside the instrument.

There's wanting to be done, to cut
the singer from his song.
And there's desire. Along an edge
we are to act the moment as the last,

reporting from the frontier of the self
all present and correct a tale to tell –
the rambling message of ourselves,
the target of our swift arithmetic.

Where at the line's end will be death,
the swiftest answer to the shortest prayer
with a daft sense of humour and bad grammar
repeating himself *death death.*

And all the bloody mess to think about,
the insurance and the weeping,
the fact the sentence came to nothing,
even those we loved were strangers.

2

Therefore I shall befriend the razor
stolen from the rare book room in Ohio,
sharp as intelligence that never learns,
keen and as I am quick to the thiefwork.

Observe his grace that fits the hand,
the curve of finger grip and shaft,
the steel arc of a wing to nowhere,
and all his speech a single syllable.

I fear the blood. I fear the moon
bruised in all the sea for his ego.
I fear the man I meet at morning
in the mirror's frame, as he fears me.

His eyes that meet me in the glass,
what do they know? I glimpse him
in the blade's glance, so carefully
his other hand shaves his Adam's apple.

His eyes catch mine but nothing's said.
Some days we hold the razor well apart
and stare each other eye to eye a time
but what we know we know and cannot say.

We shrug. That moment's all we share
along the sharp edge of reflection,
a pair of borrowed blades who meet
to carve our separate faces from the air.

The final blessing on the suicides.
The sickle at his ancient labour
cutting through the blood the air's
immediately filled with and the light gone.

I clean the cut. I stop the blood
and wipe my blue eyed double's face.
I fold the blade back in the shaft. I put
the shaft back in the box still priced $2.00.

The wanderer Yakob

*Three things always threaten a man's peace
and one before the end overthrows his mind:
illness or age or the edge of vengeance.*
THE SEAFARER

Yakob she sings, *Yakob*: his name
in her mouth in the new tongue
she knows now she knows him:
the dreamer, the wanderer, Yakob.

All this life he complains
searching for wells. He's away
shepherding across the mountains
into Andalusia, all summer long.

Driven by necessity, happenstance
one way, heartsease another,
always at adversity's far edge,
gone into everything he's scared of.

*

Torn apart, as were the valleys
to be the way they are. Thereafter
everywhere he looks it is her face,
her hands that meet across his flesh.

What's given them before the ground?
He finds the prickly pear's legacy
months after, its spines invisible
in his skin. She is a photograph.

They are as always: scarred, flawless,
stained by each other, a sketch
one moment makes in the next
in other zones the heart has.

*

Either he bad mouth misfortune
or whinge or sing supper, laugh
or clap hands for Charlie, dancing
to the flute's quick currency.

Let him begin with nothing much.
Relatively harmless he will end
relatively legless, his piss
a glitter dancing on a stone.

So far away he's vanishing, drunk
knocking at her dream's door,
his echo smothered in the canyon,
on its rim his speck of shadow.

*

He will be back he writes her,
over the border, stepping
the Earth's meridians, gipsy,
horseman turned trader.

Master of tarmac, his shotgun
under his shoulder. Thief.
With a skin or two to sell,
Navajo rings, combs, watches.

And a coat worn but the once.
In men's nature he writes her
*hunting with dogs or herding
lowland to upland, moving.*

*

A gambling man, dice and a fancy
Italian deck in his waistcoat.
A salesman with his patents,
survivor on his silver tongue.

Comic. Piano player. Drifter
with the railroads, poacher
of other men's work and women,
on the moon's tack, a migrant.

Or takes to the sea's roads,
a carpenter, bright tools
in a box made him shipman
twice round the world's rim.

*

Busker to the subway come winter,
wild geese or Cape May. Mechanic,
mercenary, preacher, poet
or magician, all come sweet April

attend the spring wind's message
warm on cheeks: *Thanne longen
folk to goon*, the pale forsythia
yellowing the landscape.

Moiré of railings again. Water
willowed, still, aloof in motion,
townspeople shimmer on a bridge,
the high jets cutting X on all.

*

War's ruckus took off many.
Some a bird bore, born again
to a season of Jesus, in fear
as he is for the night coming.

Others mad or went wasted,
some glimpsed in the mirrors
in the cold country of cocaine,
one he knew flew from a window.

Death's usual doings. *The dead
knowing nothing but through us
always inviting us in. I
who am crazy sing in their faces.*

*

Yakob in the desert: the sun
striking its single note, all day
the Panzers crisscross tracks.
Thereafter rheum and the prickly heat.

Thereafter a new name and a gammy leg.
No man endures distance unchanged.
In his sleep grey columns of smoke
advance along the night wing.

Fighting thunder and cactus.
He recalls: a following wind
and fair weather. Writes her name
in the tall sand's side: *Rachel.*

*

Yakob wakes in the city, Chicago
traffic or Moon Township, counts
bird, water, metal, his trades
always taking him town after town.

In the neon her name blinks,
in the glimpsed passing of graves,
among trucksides and storefronts,
a chain round the vagabond's wrist.

Beauty a feather, the lark's life
indecipherable. The road to Wide Ruin
wet without rain, dark without night,
and all the AM stations fading out.

*

So each day his gob's given
grievance's assonance, chant
to complaint's counterpoint:
tribulations of marriage and money.

Years blunt and brief, beyond
worse uncertainty, his mind
in its narrowing margin remarks
in his time stars haven't moved.

Yet makes him some song of it.
Shapes it for telling. The blues
and the dark colours his cries
among towns he is travelling.

*

Whiteness scribbles his scalp,
winters enter his face, a map
to the freeways, the bone
in his breast burns homeward.

The continents clutter, fenced
from the border to Santa Fé,
and all the Spanish coasts
hazy with condos and hi-rise.

If home there be and his name
still known there. If his eyes
long staring at bulkhead
and sea bile be not star blind.

*

Yakob on the home stretch,
dreaming warm grey bread, his name
along the wind in women's songs
imagines places of arrival, home.

Tales there'd be told there
by lamplight and the dark rioja,
a wineglass franking the table,
the wind's twist to the chimney.

Wishes, horses, stables, bolts.
There's no home but the roads,
smokey longings for the distance,
stones that curve along the canyon.

c

On the swings

to the far fall of my own weight
that carries me there, east, west,
over the city between the prison
and the place I come from, go to:

either's a moment pausing itself
on a rope's end, all of me there for it.
Then home watching TV: *don't make
damn all of a difference* the boy says

to the camera *in nick or not.*
All this here as the lens eye pans
bleak cements of the buildings,
the units opened once by a princess –

All this is prison. Myself I want
to be me and be useful and not be
where I'm somebody's social problem
and time's the whole sentence.

AS IT HAPPENS

This Prison is a House of Care
A Grave for Man Alive
A Touch Stone to Thee Friend
No Place for Man to Thrive

– inscription, York County Jail, dated 1820

For the lost boys, sleepless:

The usual sniggering on the stairs,
and from the night park the shrill
peacock scream might be rape or mankilling,
pierced rat or some tortured innocent.

No one calls the cops. I don't.
The night somehow goes on, whatever riddle
the owl alone in wet rainy leaves
knows the answer to. I don't,

don't sleep or awake each night dream
the same black, the same trains
made up in the yards, last word
of a late argument, the door slammed

in the house of green ginger

where I'm banged up inside as if dreaming
the dream shut tight and I never get out.
So wide was my journey.

In the dark yellow hive I'm in with the bees
where the last man out was a spy for Russia
dreaming of wings on the fourth iron walkway
of D Wing: cell by cell in its socket,
the bolts home early, the smug keys
sleeping it off, the late shift at the spyhole
counts each man alone, and there's no honey.

In my room as it happens I've a view
east over wire and the wind and the wall
to the nurse's home and the city beyond –

the remembered city

Camberwell Clerkenwell Muswell a haze,
glassy steel etched on tile was the city,
its traffic clear over to Canning Town
where I don't want to go as it happens
by wheel or by water. Wind blows there
through the towers, the spraycan sneers
this is white man's land and the shadow
on scrapyards is soon rain, it's forever
the mean meridian of Greenwich, coming in
off the flyover to Rathbone and Silvertown:
all the lost boys hunched on their knives –
the Posse, the Firm, the Little Silver Snipers

in the flats, flat voices

betwixt traffic and trains, boats on the tide,
dog grunts and the midnight rain between blocks –
upright streets as it happens, the lift shrieks
at the seventeenth floor in the airshaft
the wind hunts ruins to howl through,
the doors open on blue video voices.

You hear glass split, long clatter of heels
on the stairwell, a man's shout and a slam
all the way to the street where a car
coughs like a baby.
                            Later you hear
through the breezeblock *it's not her
car as it happens, it's not his baby.*

Elsewhere, the same night:

'You in there. Beast on the wing.
You're not my brother.

Not since you buggered my sister
chopped up my mother and stole
all my father's blessing,
dressed in another animal's skin.

You bastard. Go sleep in the desert
with a stone for your pillow
and dream if you will your dream
of a shining ladder of angels.

Jacob. Given a blade and a half oz,
I'll kill you.'

As it happens

the lost boys are playing their music,
one with a flute one a knife one a pistol,
keeping rhythm in the dark flexing muscles,
some like the dead in their stone jackets,
all serving time in the orchestra's beat
to the unfinished murderous music of men
so far below salt. Time is what it is.

As for me I was making the myth of myself
I'd come to prefer in the authorised version
fair copy and carbons security cleared
with the censor's approval, years ago
with my mates on the Bendy Rd when the world said

do this for me daddy

I love you

you owe me

38

you owe me

as it happens it happens I forgot myself,
what I knew of distance receding away
into more of itself to Cyprus and Woolwich.
Some feeling is too much already I think,

so much we can feel belongs to the gods
who are sulking, thin water our prayers
through their hands, what with the river's tale
and my shadow there small by my father's.

So much for childhood: grey boulders
the dale's length, the rainbow's high arc
and the river's fast speech that runs
through my life now. That was no dream

it happens

nor am I awake nor am I asleep now
in the walled city, the boy in me still
bawling for love, and in me the animal
prowling, and the shadow of my shadow,
and the man I am sometimes a glimpse of
almost half human again, so where am I?

Where on the road was I distracted again
no doubt by love when whatever was hunting
through her eyes met in mine what I hunted
then down the landscape, the small firs
thinning off to the valley, the flaw
in the rocky distance far snow on Mt Taylor?

Talking with the censor

In me someone believes the tale I tell
to distract from the night's terror:
diversions, dreams I don't wake from.
'I want some place to be I'm not a problem.'

Love forgive me I speak of dark things,
men's shabby concerns as to women,
through the sad nights of the masturbators,
the fist always closed on the self.

Some days I meet monsters, men I encounter
in the house of green ginger, in myself
as it happens, drawn up or caught short
with my father's lost knife in my hand.

My father with two knives

One he found shining in a furrow,
red amber, bright German steel
fallen from the sky, a blade grooved
to thread air in a man's blood.

In a cold white room I recall him
staring that knife down all Sunday,
his one thought to be done, and I,
eight, at the curtain's lace edge.

His pocket knife I keep: bone black,
brass head, bird's eye for a rivet
sighting the lifted beak of the blade –
useful and home made as he was.

Like him plain and of little speech,
given to blunt surgery on sheep
or whittling sticks any weather
out on the hill's side, long ago now.

Towards daylight:

all this and the rain's endurance
Lady I've aged, maybe you've aged me.
What I wanted: to roost in the nest
in the dark tree of your body.

I'd live alone but who would I tell,
alone as it happens. From this place
months go looking for years and hands
for each other and night after night

your voice on the tape in my skull
pauses for breath, breathes, speaks
your name with my own, as it happens,
as I grow old thinking of you.

The bee dance

Let the grey dust thicken on the landings,
let the spiders tick in the wall,
let the locks rust and the keys be lost.

This is the yellow hive of my skull
where the bees dance on the honeycomb
their tales of direction and distance.

They tell how high the sun is, how far
to sweet marjoram, borage and thyme,
and the tall green masts of the sunflowers.

Cain's songs

If there's a tune no one remembers.
The words fall away and the voice
remembers in bits, trailing out –

> *O when you loved me*
> *When the wind in a garden*
> *When the carousel*

In our songs innocence comes back,
our childhood some moment a throstle
sang in the orchard at day's end,
you sat among blossoms and moths.

> *O when you loved me.*
> *Till with love's fury I came*
> *to murderer's home.*

Don't I know you? Did we meet
when last time you were victim,
I the persecutor? Maybe.

> *For the prosecution:*

I arrested him.
His reply was
I've got nothing to say.

He then said *Answer me truthfully officer*
how many pubs in Weymouth
am I not banned from?

I said *None sir.*
It was 9.10 p.m.

Here's a man with a hammer
banging the sound under his fist.
The sound grows as it travels,
dies down its wavelength.

Maybe that's his wife he's beating,
beating with a hammer. Maybe
with the nails between his teeth
and the hand and the hammer raised up.

Maybe her. Maybe him. Maybe me.

Where love stays. Where
there are no prisons, no police.
That world you speak of, friend,
lives in another song in a tune
I can't recall, another tale
told at the road's turn where wind
moves among beeches. I know.
I was there. The wind told me.

Grieving the years out.
I have made a room in the wind
where the days grow tired of each other.

It is a weepy sound, my grief
but it is not weeping. Harsh,
it is not anger with anyone.

So wide was my journey.
The moon shines on the sea,
it does not intend to.

For the boys on the wing

They are birds some thought free once
on the wind's swing and air's drop.
Hours perched on the landing railings
to be locked up to be glimpsed
among bars and the meshed stale air,
sometimes singing, their wings tucked.

We are entering silence,
cloud closing the room's light
and the radio music suddenly graver,
each in his moment twoed-up
or threed or alone with the brickwork
hours, nights, years, sinners
whose proper life study is silence.

As ever: half a world hungry
and the deployments continued, the swift
planetary surgery closer, it seems
not a damn thing we can dance to.

Forgive me directness,
And the president his blindness.
And the chairman his bullshitski.

Black and white with my own money.
So far they can't make my space less.
Round and round anti-clockwise my project
silence but who would I say it to?

Between this ear and this ear I'm free.
So tell them, whose task is to despise me,
whose career to contain me, tell them
who call this hell we live here.

Outside I was always
looking round for them –
chancers, dancers, addicts
of the dark. So roundly

all these are cursed men
by their lovers, victims,
consensus of the deceased,
and forever. *Worthy,*

worthy of praising
one sings of his Jesus,
another finding at mass
the priest's hands moving

a moment of beauty,
his vernacular a holy
rigmarole tale told of
bread, wine, blood.

Think of Billy. He'll not wince
past the checkout. Think of John
overdue in the remembering department,
in the red to the last lost quid
hidden in his shoe and that owing
to Veiled Threats Associates. He recalls
a whole ocean cut to a wind and two blues.
He has pictures to prove it: the hills,
the harebells whipped by the first
wind of September. Love I remember:
you were fierce, you persisted
through whatever the weather was.

Born again to the wind's tap on brick.
Born again to the island of the self,
the same giggle in the orchestra pit,
nights when the snake of her dark voice
slides over me. She says all journeys
have no returns. The radio sings
She & I don't go to the laundrette no more.
Here's tansy the dried deathless flower,
roses fallen on roots and I'm Orfus
the man who has everything calling back
from the border and lost her forever,
bringing no light back from the dead.

Think of Az. Az says in the
prison of the self he was born to
he's been here there and Zimbabwe,
the wire and the wall notwithstanding.

What he feels that he feels is always
dissolving. Let's say he matured late
or tripped on the wrong foot, he was
victim victim, his luck never ran in.

Though it's no excuse some days
he's the brain of a squeegee mop,
he says *You make the decisions, so now
You figure it out: what to do with me.*

Don't say guilt, don't say innocent.
Suspend disbelief. Say *the convicted*.
Say *the problem of male violence*.
The problem of abstraction, e.g.
freedom. Some went abroad
to meet a bullet, some take
the tube train's last amendment,
some sleep with the rain and a knife,
spiders caught in each other's webs.

So wide was my journey, like the bees.
We have no wings, our honey bitter,
sour as green ginger, and for so much time
we make little at our trades at the
sewing machine at the sewing machine
with the needle eyes rising and rising.
Social or solitary we're bees, we dance
without partners or sense of direction.
We have silence. We have the many eyes
of mosaic vision. And this herb.
This herb destroys worms. Wormwood.

My footsteps come to the page edge.
I glimpse him again, my violent father,
knee deep in the landscape
till he'd had enough of it. Him
with all the other closed books
whose covers are soil, stone,
the long weeds by the allotments.
I close him again for the last time.

So far to the wall to count bricks.
So we've a rich inner life have we?
What I want is Gloucester Rd Anyplace.
Single. What I want is trains,
and my face angled in wind, my hat
blown away behind. I want to be
in other bars asking what's this game
called *Family Tissues*, what to do
with these blank folded sheets?
I want rain, the lamefoot doves
crowding city monuments, the traffic
and the grainy flush of air in the tubes.

What the righteous don't know

They think only hot and cold
and the dark we fall through.
They don't know life goes on in hell
where there's work painting the brick,
maintaining the fabric, in the kitchens
preparing the devil's marvellous picnics.
We've a roof over our heads,
three squares and it's steady
if promotion comes slow. What
the righteous don't know:
we're their shadows,
wherever they are in the light.

Bodies

Some whose eyes I don't meet,
hands I don't shake, one that cut
NF in a man's back and left him
choke on his testicles, the knife
still in him and ran with the video.

Some with no story to bring sleep
or get supper and no tale
travellers repeat. He can say
I was responsible, can't say
I killed her, shot her, took an axe
and cut her to pieces, sawed her up
with the breadknife we'd used
so many years cutting our bread.

He asks himself over and over
what name her teeth had bit back
in her long coming, her *tsunami*
she called it in the pluperfect.
How when he'd phoned she was
never at home so where was she?

*

Charged with looking at the building.
In evidence a white male in a dark Allegro.
Some with a bottle, some with a needle.

Late afternoon the white meat waggons
roll in the day's catch, remanded
without bail, some misfit, some vicious,
the accused to be numbered.

D

*

Chalkie White, Metal Mickey, Spider Webb,
so where be they now? Last seen
with Murphy of Shepherd's Bush Boots,
helping Sgt E.C.T. Brainfuck from Paddington Green.
Last heard of on the block, on the book,
on the muffin run to Brixton.

Just helping Bill with his enquiries.

This one's Bungalow: no top storey.
This one's Muzz. And this one
singing in the canteen clatter at noon
I'm nobody's child, I'm nobody's child.
And no wonder another voice calls
down the wing as the neon hush falls
across paperwork and it's two hours
to unlock in the empire of the chinagraph.

Time to reflect:
                    he hit her with a bottle,
a sewing machine, a chair, a tennis racket.
Offered her the easy way with aspirin.
Hit her twice when once was twice enough.

At the centre of the labyrinth: a rose.
At the centre of the rose's labyrinth: a worm.

Timekeeper

It doesn't get worse
It just goes on being bad

As ever on the digital
all the seconds my life
I repeat one by one I
repeat myself: *so wide*
was my journey. As ever
no one to tell it to
whatever lies I write
between the barred lines
on the page in the upright
iron of these letters, who
to send them in any case?
What we do here is count,
count, pencil in, turning
a smooth choreography – arm,
chain, keys, whistle, Whisky
2 on the walkietalkie, slam
of the great gates shut –
a century, more. Oh
you'll see me dance, some
time you'll hear me sing,
truth is we despise as we
count each other, as we
study the clock's time
ticking *knockback knockback*,
the hours one by one on Sir
and as ever it's a long time
to the next number 9 bus and this
urgent news out of nowhere.

I threw my blade.
It was a lucky shot.
It got him right off.
It killed him.
Or it was a unlucky shot.
I been here six years.

How divide how many ways
cut up time, alone, paring
the fingernail, notching
the calendar, shaving
a match to a match stick
by stick to his Romany cart,
wherein he would sail
any lane as he chose
or the slow wind suggested?
The days anti-clockwise
walking the yard count
how many miles, how much rain
and what names for the birds
which are two being *hawk,*
sparrowhawk, sparrow?
Each man here is a thread,
each man is a needle
stitching his tale told
silently over, already old.
Young as I am in this place
whispers run through me,
nightcries, feet running
and rumours. So I moved
once back in the old life
through cities of women's
remembrance and men's yarns
where my name is a ghost,
face barely recalled. Now
my road's closed I've years
to prepare, to polish,
rehearse my story for someone,
anyone, no one, myself then.

The man I killed. I don't
regret it: I'd kill him again.
But for a long time I'd look
at the stars through the window
and I'd see his face.

Through the judas you'll
see me reading or sleeping
or staring into nothing
at a gesture's midpoint,
all my private dancing
in public. Once more
I free the bird my heart
in the closed 8 by 12
our space is, she and I.
She sings. She wakes me
and flies at the little panes,
the yellow paint, the brick.
Beyond glass and the wire
of razor hair and stars,
traffic and the wind. They
make the sound a sea breaks
on beaches and the risen
crowd's roar in the stadium
up on its toes. This side,
just me and the budgie,
lost as though long steering
by one star quit the sky.
Asleep I dreamed my heart
the dark star far away
I long for and remember,
all the stones between us.
I tell her *no* and tear
the star out of my chest,
don't you ever come see me.

At the solstice

As for me I'm free to ponder the crow
my voice blent in the day's wind
soft grey at my back. To the east
stumpy London humming to itself
blocks spires over the land's hump
distant finger of the Telecom tower
my needle's eye of the city my
marker for Baker Street. Out
on some errand some long ago want
for an open country talking out loud
with no one to hear. My good days
are like this one into another just
getting about with an arm and a leg
two of each if I'm lucky. Lucky I am
with my notes my keys to the prison
I pass in and out I sing for my supper.
It could be otherwise. Years back
in the paranoid self of myself
I recall in the seventyeight of it all
I would have killed a man and been here
meeting myself a prisoner on no road
anywhere a record no one listens to
a book no one reads any more my gear
out of style all the jokes out of date.
Years in the dark mad half mad
what would we say when the weather
no longer matters the time the time
any day what month what the season
what game to play? Spot the psychopath.
Which man kills because he feels nothing
and which when he never felt more
which for gain which revenge to be done
which accident which innocent as charged?

What to say when the fear the blood
down the thickening tunnel the cave
the thump in the head the chest
the heart's labouring pump drums nights
at the temple second by second
systole by dystole its promise
a last *jessica jessica* fading off
on the cardiogram's blipless quiet
unplugged at the wall next customer
caught in the panic that kills
bolting from bed 3.00 a.m. in the soft
city's groan at the window the clock's
even passing of time the birds
before dawn the light's blue glaze
in your sleeping face love I begin
I start saying goodbye my wave of the sea.

Wormwood I grew. Tall in the feathering wind
in my garden all summer taller the next
a pushy green bush small yellow cushions
a dusting of air. Wormwood you drew me.
Bitter plant. Absinthe and illusion.
Beer made in the name of this district
there's none now an oak forest once
scrub clearing last feeding of sheep
before market. The long trains
put on speed west go crying to Bristol
to Plymouth the rocky rainy peninsulas.
Crows rubbery avuncular here in the mist
in the grass small peppermint snails.
Wormwood the name of the prison its wall
a pit dug in men's lives four hulks
four ships that never sail anywhere
moored in time in a dead space
between the wire and the wall.
The name *Wormwood* the star falling
destroys a third part of the waters
the third part of men. Goodbye heartsease.

In the nowhere waiting for a result
hanging on to the empty urine bottle
hoping for anything the bomb to drop
the knife to its tryst in the artery.
In the shadow land. And overhead
a helicopter in the broody air of August
above the keen abstractions and the facts
that are all bricks locks razor wire.
We fail as men where is no centre
to the self, these many voices
failing in first person singular.
I've done two rapes a man whispers
but I'm here under another name.
I'm no father confessor. Here I am
too many shades of blue already
in the three ring circus of myself
thinking maybe I can hide in here
with all the other confessions
in my study of male violence
but I can't. No more dancing
for this customer. No more
crossing town to drink Campari
with the daughters of the brown contessa.
Time to say goodbye to the dark ladies.
Here is where we leave the shoes.
Here is where we leave the gloves
the hat the 44 the rolled umbrella.
We're pulling in your licence Jimmy.

Bricks made of clay. Clay dug
in the river leas in the Thames flood plain
brick cut fired tapped to the trowel
coursed brick on brick making prison.
Prisoners brickies once labourers
thieves from the bridewell hard men
from the Millwall to dig in the mud
their own quarters the cells
of all who came after men women
convicted walking the yard circles
turning the mill hooded and ruled
by silence. Boxed masked ranked

of a Sunday sly in the cubicled church
passing notes looking always front
at priest and their maker condemned
to brood on their criminal ways
they step in a chained procession
down time cuffed censored banged up
there is nothing to hope for. Bricks.

Worm's Wood I invent. Old dark place
under the treecover of oak and sycamore
bushy scree tangle of briar thornwood
men are lost in. Wood of *straunge wormes*
snagging men's ghosts caught earthbound
in the ongoing assault that is prison
the failed university of time the first
last faith called fear. Everything
sharp blades fists in the recess
a kicking an ear bitten off here's
an edge takes an eye a finger a pencil
a razorblade jammed in a toothbrush.
And no maps no signs again no way out
each shadow casting its shadow.
My journey can end here I can
die be forgotten lie unconsoled
in the brown city clay any time
a fate common reasonable even so what?
I could be anyone the wood-goer Nick
I have almost a name for him *Nick*
who moves in out the nightmares
down the landings of the sleepers
sleepless fingering the dreams
the convicted whisper each celled
dark bricked barred lonely alone
forever maybe lost most likely
I could be him: say Nicholas Wildman
a fox for instance the very same man
John known as Marsbar alias Professor
a.k.a. Jack be Nimble Jack be Quick.

The night whispers

for John and all the men in the world called John

1

There was a friend of mine,
used to offer me a cigarette.
On a Tuesday. John was talking.
He was saying what he hears, his ear
pressed along the wall along the wing.
Time's all there is he says, flat,
to one side, every second word
what he'll never do again with women.
He'll take a light off me though.

He's the man that ate boiled ham raw.
He'll take on a sliced loaf single handed.
Time is the crease in his pants I think,
pressed as in the army under the mattress.
John keeps himself neat. He knows
how quick they'll spirit him away
in a bodybag along the stairs before unlock.
He says he heard the screw say *One Off Sir.*

It's time.

Time he looks back from morning after morning,
his face changing in the same mirror.
Time is the razorblade, the comb's teeth
and the measure of the toothpaste. Time he eats,
shits, drinks, is sometimes merry in,
the fallen grey he lifts off his shoulder.

Time scuffs the shoe and blunts all the nails.
If there were no nights there'd be no fear.
Time I could handle but all this dark stuff
either side between the light and the light.

Time is what.
Time is.

He tells me what he hears in the night whispers
through pipework and brickwork, bars and the hard gloss,
and he writes down the messages: *Oddy's on the roof.*
The nurses are having a party. It's in.
All it costs are little pictures of the Queen.

Oh and love he says. *Love Love Love's*
faint echo on the landings, through the masonry
on a thin late airwave *Love* running down the batteries,
singing on a bent guitar
Lost in the saddle again.

Ah, John.

Lost in time both of us talking about love,
a word born over again and again in the prison house
where so many with their hands killed love,
and then the dark came down forever. So now
behind the yellow wall and the yellow fence
where the wind in a scatter of old leaves
beats the wire to security, the dogs howl
moonward and the champion dopesniffer Duke
sleeps on but John when he sleeps never dreams.

Time is what it is. The protagonist is mad again,
lost in some mean southern border town
all barber shops and bars and far too many shoes.
I've been out again beating my heart on the wind,
and maybe this time John we never get home
and the journey ends here and time's all there is.

The idea is don't die in prison John,
in this part of the nightmare.

2

My brother calls me from the world's other side
and never said which city. He's been robbed,
he's broke, homeless, out of a job and 48,
he's drunk in the wrong house and whose phone is it
and I fear my brother will die in the wind.
He says he's glad dirty money from a dirty job
went to a dirty place to buy a dirty girl junk.
Wherever morning is I hope he'll still be glad.
He'll send an address when he has one.

So now you know the plot. Fox is away
in Australasia waiting for the cops,
and when he called I was thinking about John
and what he tells me: *many things*
will never happen. As for me
I've been too close too long to the damned
and can't leave, lost as they are in time,
on my wordtrack covering the territory,
always in the dark thinking I've a lucifer
when I'm far too near the wire when the lights go up
and I'm lost in the saddle again.

Take me home, love, my scars and all my alibis
and my bad manners and whatever wounds we die of.
If you can find me. My name is John.
Maybe you can love what will be left of me.
Take me out of this prison.

Carteret Plage
(for Judi)

I came to tell you my feather:
at the marina so many bells,
so many voices coming ashore
saying *listen we have nothing*
to say beyond who we are:
old business the wind works
through the slack riggings
of boats laid up for winter,
each the one note clapped
on the incoming wind, slap
of metal on mast, wave on hull,
rope on the rain an orchestra
of random notes moored where
always this was the river,
for someone the waters of home.

My blue feather. On the beach
so many lives feathered into being
and out of it. And so much
interesting foreign detritus
in the rubbery scourings
in the kelp's piled tripes
weary with flies in summer.
Everywhere a tangle of guts,
crabs, starfish and bladderwrack,
the weeds of abandoned brains,
tumours, dropped masks, amputations
and all the bloody murders ever
ending in string, ripped nets,
hooks, driftwood and the wreck
of the good ship *One blue glove*

Quatre-vingt je ne sais quoi,
Merde de lapin s.v.p. Ce poisson-çi,
c'est une seule nucléare n'est-ce pas?
Mes enfants, ma langue c'est fini,
je suis en vacances, après la guerre,
not permitted to be bored or to work.
Mine is a country of small cheeses,
here I live in a bordello of cheese
and white Muscadet with the widow
of Arromanches, perhaps I'm a man
other men would like to be like
but they keep their distance,
ces enfants que le bonheur oublie.
It's late *et la clef c'est fini*
dans la chambre privée,
et Monsieur Toledo bonne nuit.

My blue feather. Falling.
In the quick wind. If the wind
turn you round, blow you west
down the rowdy Atlantic
and out of yourself, my bride,
my blue feather. By night
on the dark edge of water
I hold you consulting my text
that says here *a wise man*
holds out. Do we think
the rock thinks forming the slow
thought of itself that dissolves?
The wind off the sea, steady.
On the quays faces of Vikings,
on the beach wayward paths
secretly marked by stones,
by the track of a dog,
the snake tongue of seaweed
spelling your name in cursive
in a scribble of wormcasts,
and the doll's burst head,
from her bleached broken face
a single blue eye staring seaward.

Ken Smith was born in 1938 in Rudston, East Yorkshire, the son of an itinerant farm labourer. He has worked in Britain and in America as a teacher, freelance writer, barman, magazine editor, potato picker and BBC reader, and has held writing fellowships at Leeds University, Kingston Polytechnic and Clark University and Holy Cross, Worcester, Massachusetts. From September 1985 to August 1987 he was writer-in-residence at Wormwood Scrubs prison. He lives in London.

Smith's first book, *The Pity*, was published by Jonathan Cape in 1967, and his second, *Work, distances/poems*, by Swallow Press, Chicago in 1972. Poems from these two collections and from numerous other books and pamphlets published between 1964 and 1980 (including *Fox Running*) were brought together in his Bloodaxe Selected, *The Poet Reclining* (1982). In 1986 his collection *Terra* was made a Poetry Book Society Recommendation and was also shortlisted for the Whitbread Prize. His latest books are *A Book of Chinese Whispers* (1987), his collected prose, and *Wormwood*, which is a Poetry Book Society Recommendation for Autumn 1987.